How Are Climate and Weather Different?

HOUGHTON MIFFLIN HARCOURT

PHOTOGRAPHY CREDITS: COVER (bg) ©Don Farrall/PhotoDisc/Getty Images; 3 (bg) ©Tetra Images/Alamy Images; 5 (t) Corbis; 6 (b) ©Stephen Morris/Getty Images; 7 (t) ©djgis/Shutterstock; 8 (b) ©Image Source/Superstock; 9 (t) ©Don Farrall/PhotoDisc/Getty Images; 10 (t) ©Krys Bailey/Alamy Images; 11 (b) ©Design Pics Inc./Alamy Images; 13 (t) ©MELBA PHOTO AGENCY/Alamy; 14 (t) ©Corbis; 15 (l) ©Alamy Images; 15 (r) ©Corbis; 16 (b) ©JH Pete Carmichael/Riser/Getty Images; 17 (t) ©Stefan Huwiler/Imagebroker/Corbis; 19 (t) ©falk/Shutterstock; 21 (b) ©Stockbyte/Getty Images

ISBN: 978-0-544-07354-8

3 4 5 6 7 8 9 10 1083 21 20 19 18 17 16 15 14

4500470080   A B C D E F G

Be an Active Reader!

Look at these words.

atmosphere	precipitation	equator
water cycle	runoff	latitude
evaporation	weather	climate zone
condensation	climate	

Look for answers to these questions.

Where is water on Earth's surface?

What is the water cycle?

How do the sun, ocean, and atmosphere affect each other?

What is changing weather like?

What is climate?

What affects climate?

Where are climate zones located?

How do climate zones affect living things?

Have climates always been the same?

How is climate different from weather?

Where is water on Earth's surface?

Earth is often called the "water planet." When you consider that about 70% of Earth's surface is covered in water, it's no wonder that Earth has been given this nickname. The oceans contain most of the water on the planet. There is also water in lakes, rivers, ponds, streams, glaciers, and marshes all over the world. There's even underground water.

The water in Earth's oceans is salt water. Fresh water sources are glaciers, ponds, streams, and most lakes and rivers. Both salt water and fresh water play an essential role in the condition of the atmosphere, the mixture of gases, dust, and small particles of matter that surrounds Earth.

The salt water of the oceans covers most of Earth's surface.

What is the water cycle?

Earth's water is not limited to the surface of Earth. Water is also in the atmosphere in the form of water vapor. Water vapor is water in its gas state. You can't see this water, but it becomes part of a continuously moving process on Earth's surface called the water cycle. The water cycle is the process in which water continuously moves from Earth's surface into the atmosphere and back again. It describes the relationship between water in the ocean, on land, and in the atmosphere. It's a natural recycling process of water that has been occurring for ages. Water in the ocean or in a puddle may have been going through the water cycle for millions of years.

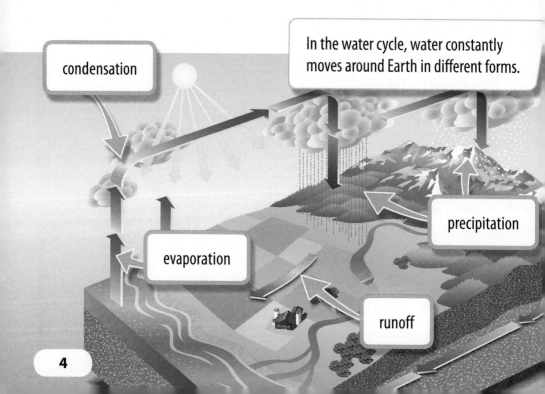

condensation

In the water cycle, water constantly moves around Earth in different forms.

precipitation

evaporation

runoff

Dew on plants in the early morning is formed by condensation. Water vapor has changed back to liquid water.

As the sun heats oceans, lakes, and other water sources, an important process occurs. Heat causes the water particles to speed up and start spreading apart so that liquid water turns into water vapor, a gas. This change from liquid water into a gas is called evaporation. You see the effects of evaporation when you notice water puddles from a rainstorm drying up when the sun comes out.

When water vapor rises into the air, it may cool and change back to liquid water in a process called condensation. Condensation is the change of a gas into a liquid. In the atmosphere, this liquid water takes the form of tiny droplets that join together to form clouds. You can see the result of condensation on Earth's surface in the form of dewdrops on plants.

How do the sun, ocean, and atmosphere affect each other?

As the droplets that make up clouds continue to join together, they get heavier. The droplets fall to Earth's surface in a process called precipitation. The droplets may fall as rain, snow, sleet, or hail, depending on the air temperature.

Some precipitation goes directly into oceans, lakes, and other bodies of water. Some of it seeps into the ground, becoming groundwater. Some flows down mountains and into rivers and streams as runoff, or water that does not soak into the ground and instead flows across Earth's surface. Runoff eventually flows back into oceans and lakes.

Clouds are the result of the condensation of water vapor.

The heating of ocean water can affect the weather in areas that are far inland.

Clouds, wind, and temperature are three factors related to weather. Weather is what is happening in the atmosphere at a certain place and time. Every kind of weather—wind, rain, snow—is influenced by the sun heating ocean water, land, and air.

When ocean water interacts with the atmosphere, big changes can result. Water that is warmer than the air above it heats the air. Differences in air temperature can cause breezes to blow. As patches of air hit against each other and move, light or even strong winds can develop. Winds that start over ocean water may move over land and change the weather there.

What is changing weather like?

An important aspect of weather is temperature. Temperature has a lot to do with the kind of precipitation you will see falling from the sky. When temperatures in the atmosphere are around 0 °Celsius (°C), or 32 °Fahrenheit (°F), the precipitation that forms may be snow. However, the temperature throughout the atmosphere is uneven. The air closer to the ground may be warmer than 0 °C (32 °F), so snow may melt and become rain before it hits the ground.

Precipitation that falls from clouds when the temperature is colder than 0 °C (32 °F) may fall all the way to the ground as snow. Sleet is snow that melts as it falls through a thin layer of warm air and then refreezes into ice before reaching the ground.

Snow may fall when atmospheric temperatures are 0 °C (32 °F) or less.

Tornadoes may occur along with strong thunderstorms.

Weather can change quickly and dramatically. Cold air can move into areas of warm, moist air, causing thunderstorms to develop. When winds coming from different directions meet, they may rotate, causing a tornado. These storms can be very dangerous, moving in directions that are difficult to predict.

Hurricanes are the most powerful storms on Earth. They start as thunderstorms over warm ocean water where the air is moist and warm. The warm water evaporates. It releases energy when it condenses, providing energy to the moving winds above it. As the storm gains more energy, it becomes a tropical depression. It spirals around and slowly picks up speed as it moves. When the storm reaches high wind speeds of more than 119 kilometers (74 miles) per hour, it is a hurricane. Some hurricanes are as large as 965 kilometers (600 miles) across!

Snow is part of the long-term climate of some areas.

What is climate?

If you traveled around the United States, you'd see that there are different weather patterns in different places. It is often very rainy in the Pacific Northwest and very dry in the Southwest. The Northeast gets cold and snowy winters. These patterns go beyond the changing weather that can happen from day to day. Each of these places has a different climate. Climate is the pattern of weather an area experiences over a long period of time.

To understand the climate of a particular area, scientists study the average temperature, amount of precipitation, and wind speeds over a long period of time. Scientists must record and analyze the averages for each month over many years to determine what a climate is like.

Day-to-day changes in temperature are part of an area's weather conditions. Average temperatures during the seasons in an area determine the area's climate. For example, it is true that places near the North Pole get a lot of cold weather and snow. But it's the weather over a very long period of time that makes up the area's climate.

Some places get cold winters and hot summers, while others have somewhat even temperatures throughout the year. A very dry climate, such as a desert, may have less than 25 centimeters (10 inches) of precipitation per year. A wet climate, such as a rain forest, may have up to 6.4 meters (21 feet) of precipitation in a year.

Dry conditions are part of the long-term weather patterns of some areas.

What affects climate?

What makes one place have a different kind of climate than another? An area's distance from the equator is an important factor. The equator is an imaginary line around Earth. It divides Earth into a northern part and a southern part, and it is equally distant from the North and South Poles. The areas right around the equator are usually hot all year round. As you go north and south from the equator, average temperatures get cooler. Latitude is a measure of how far north or south a place is from the equator.

Another factor that affects climate is the distance of an area from large bodies of water. Oceans and large lakes heat and cool more slowly than places on land.

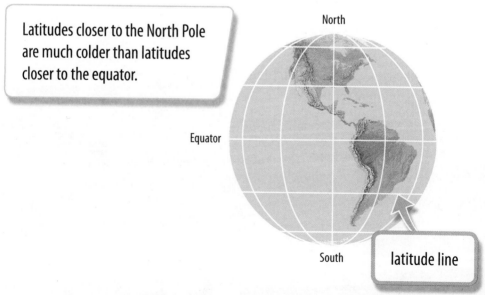

Latitudes closer to the North Pole are much colder than latitudes closer to the equator.

North

Equator

South

latitude line

The wet climate on the ocean-facing side of a mountain is caused by the movement of air off the ocean.

Ocean water near the equator is warmer than ocean water in other places on Earth. This warm water heats the air above it, causing moving water and winds that can reach around the globe. The Gulf Stream is an ocean current that affects climates. It flows up from the equator along the East Coast of North America, and across the Atlantic Ocean to northern Europe.

When air moves off the ocean and up a mountain, it creates a wet climate on the ocean-facing side. The air dries before it moves down the other side of the mountain, creating a dry climate on the other side. Climate around the world is affected by moving ocean currents and moving air.

A temperate climate receives a wide variety of changing weather.

Where are climate zones located?

If you look at a map, you will observe that areas with similar climates are located at about the same distance from the equator. A climate zone is an area that has similar average temperatures and precipitation. The climate zone closest to the equator is called the tropical climate zone, and it is the warmest. The areas closest to the North Pole and South Pole are called polar climate zones. The areas between the polar and tropical climate zones are called temperate climate zones.

Places that are in a temperate climate usually have four different seasons, each with differing temperatures. There may be individual differences between areas within a temperate climate, but the general temperatures will differ depending on each season.

The amount of direct sunlight in each climate zone plays the most important part in the temperature of each place. In a tropical climate zone, the sunlight is usually intense throughout the year. This makes temperatures in the tropical climate zone the warmest of all three zones. Even so, the amount of precipitation varies greatly between various places in the tropical climates.

In polar climates, the sunlight is not very intense, even in the summer. As a result, this zone is very cold and often covered in ice. It is also very dry. There is little precipitation in polar climate zones.

The amount of sunlight in climate zones determines their temperature.

How do climate zones affect living things?

Factors such as temperature and the amount of precipitation not only affect climate, they also affect the plants and animals that can live in an area. Each zone has specific plant and animal life that can survive in the particular conditions there.

Some areas in temperate and tropical zones have many trees and can support a lot of animal life. The animals use the trees for food and shelter.

In wet climates, many trees have leaves with tips that allow extra water to drip off them. In dry climates, many trees have leaves that hold water in them so that they can conserve, or save, the water. Plants in cold climates often grow close to the ground to have less exposure to cold.

This tropical plant, called a bromeliad, collects water in its leaves and provides a place for tiny animals to live.

The lizard can keep its body warm because the climate where it lives has high temperatures and a lot of sunlight.

Animals depend on the climate conditions of an area to help them survive. Horned lizards and sidewinder rattlesnakes, for example, live in very dry, warm climates. Their bodies require warmth and very little water to stay alive.

Other animals are suited to living in cold climates. They have thick coats of fur to protect them from the cold.

Other animals move from climate to climate during the year. Conditions of their environment make it hard for them to find food or water when the temperatures and weather conditions change.

The way animals and plants are distributed around the world has to do with the same conditions that determine climate. The average precipitation, temperature, sunlight, and wind conditions affect where living things are located.

Have climates always been the same?

The large areas of land on Earth, called continents, were once in different locations than they are today. This is because Earth's plates—large, moving areas of Earth's crust and mantle—have shifted and broken apart. An area that was once in a tropical climate zone with no ocean around it may now be in a temperate climate zone near an ocean.

Earth's plates have taken millions of years to shift and move, and the climate has also changed during that time. The plants and animals in different climate zones have also reacted to these changes.

Millions of years ago, today's continents were part of a continent called Pangaea. As areas of Pangaea moved apart, some of them moved away from the equator and some toward it. That caused their climates to change.

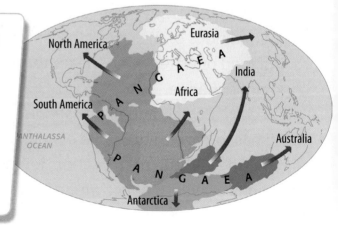

The rock layer in which a fossil is found helps tell when the organism lived. The type of organism may provide clues to what the climate was like at that time.

Scientists can see evidence that climates have changed during particular ages in the past. They have discovered this by examining plant and animal fossils in different layers of rock. The layer of the rock a particular fossil is found in tells scientists when and where that organism lived. The kinds of fossils in the rock give clues to the climate conditions during that time period. For example, if fossils of tropical plants are found in an area that is a desert today, scientists know that the area had a wet, tropical climate when the organisms were alive.

Earth has gone through long time periods when the climate was very cold. These periods, called ice ages, affected the plant and animal life on Earth.

The weather of an area changes from day to day. The climate stays the same for long periods of time.

How is climate different from weather?

The water cycle plays an important part in weather. The water cycle occurs in temperate zones as well as in polar and tropical zones. Precipitation occurs in every climate zone and in every area on Earth. The day-to-day changes in temperature, wind, and precipitation are what make up weather. The weather in one area can be different from the weather in a place just a short distance away. For example, the part of a city that's near a coast may be cloudy and cool, while an inland area less than 32 kilometers (20 miles) away may be hot and sunny. Although these areas are in the same climate zone, they may experience different weather conditions at the same time.

Remember that weather is what is happening in the atmosphere at a certain time and place. Climate is the pattern of weather an area experiences over a long period of time.

The sun is the energy source of all weather events on Earth. Sunlight warms Earth's surface. It heats ocean water, providing the energy that fuels hurricanes and tropical storms. As a diagram of the water cycle on page 4 shows, the sun's heat causes water on Earth's surface to evaporate into the atmosphere, condense into clouds, and then fall back to Earth as precipitation. The water cycle moves water between Earth's surface and the atmosphere, and will continue to affect our weather and climate conditions in the future.

The water cycle depends on interactions between the sun, the atmosphere, and Earth's surface, which includes bodies of water.

Make a Water Cycle Model

Show how the sun and ocean interact in the water cycle by making a model. Use posterboard or the shallow lid of a large box. Show the placement of oceans, land masses such as mountains, clouds, and the sun. Use cut-out arrows and labels to illustrate what happens during the processes of the water cycle. Show where evaporation, condensation, precipitation, and runoff occur during the cycle.

 Write a Comparison-Contrast

Write two paragraphs to compare and contrast weather and climate. Be sure to give specific examples of weather and climate in each paragraph.

Glossary

atmosphere [AT·muh·sfeer] The mixture of gases that surround Earth.

climate [KLY·muht] The pattern of weather an area experiences over a long period of time.

climate zone [KLY·muht ZOHN] An area that has similar average temperatures and precipitation throughout.

condensation [kahn·duhn·SAY·shuhn] The process by which a gas changes into a liquid.

equator [ee·KWAY·ter] An imaginary line around Earth, equally distant from the North and South Poles.

evaporation [ee·VAP·uh·ray·shuhn] The process by which a liquid changes into a gas.

latitude [LAT·ih·tood] A measure of how far north or south a place is from the equator.

precipitation [pree·sip·uh·TAY·shuhn] Water that falls from clouds to Earth's surface.

runoff [RUHN•awf] Water that does not soak into the ground and instead flows across Earth's surface.

water cycle [WAW•ter SY•kuhl] The process in which water continuously moves from Earth's surface into the atmosphere and back again.

weather [WETH•er] The condition of the atmosphere at a certain place and time.